W9-AGZ-068

Jun'22 3 / 1 /0

NICARAGUA

HONDURAS

Puerto Cabezas

Coco River

Ocotal

Somoto

Gulf of Fonseca

NICARAGUA

River

Prinzapolka

Estelí   Jinotega

Matagalpa

Rio Grande   *de Matagalpa*

Chinandega

Lake Managua

León   Boaco

Tipitapa   Juigalpa

Bluefields

Managua

Granada

Jinotepe

Lake Nicaragua

N
W   E
S

Rivas   *Isla de Ometepe*

PACIFIC OCEAN   *CARIBBEAN SEA*

San Carlos

San Juan River

0   25   50 Miles
0   25   50 Kilometers
Albers Conic Equal-Area Projection

COSTA RICA

87W   86W   85W   04W

15N

14N

13N

12N

11N

DISCOVERING
CENTRAL AMERICA
History, Politics, and Culture

NICARAGUA

Charles J. Shields

Mason Crest
Philadelphia

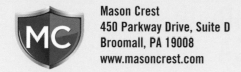

Mason Crest
450 Parkway Drive, Suite D
Broomall, PA 19008
www.masoncrest.com

©2016 by Mason Crest, an imprint of National Highlights, Inc.

Printed and bound in the United States of America.

CPSIA Compliance Information: Batch #DCA2015.
For further information, contact Mason Crest at 1-866-MCP-Book.

First printing
1 3 5 7 9 8 6 4 2

Library of Congress Cataloging-in-Publication Data
on file at the Library of Congress

ISBN: 978-1-4222-3291-0 (hc)
ISBN: 978-1-4222-8657-9 (ebook)

Discovering Central America: History, Politics, and Culture series ISBN: 978-1-4222-3284-2

DISCOVERING CENTRAL AMERICA: History, Politics, and Culture

Belize
Central America: Facts and Figures
Costa Rica
El Salvador

Guatemala
Honduras
Nicaragua
Panama

Table of Contents

KEY ICONS TO LOOK FOR:

Words to Understand: These words with their easy-to-understand definitions will increase the reader's understanding of the text, while building vocabulary skills.

Sidebars: This boxed material within the main text allows readers to build knowledge, gain insights, explore possibilities, and broaden their perspectives by weaving together additional information to provide realistic and holistic perspectives.

Research Projects: Readers are pointed toward areas of further inquiry connected to each chapter. Suggestions are provided for projects that encourage deeper research and analysis.

Text-Dependent Questions: These questions send the reader back to the text for more careful attention to the evidence presented there.

Series Glossary of Key Terms: This back-of-the book glossary contains terminology used throughout this series. Words found here increase the reader's ability to read and comprehend higher-level books and articles in this field.

Discovering Central America

James D. Henderson

CENTRAL AMERICA is a beautiful part of the world, filled with generous and friendly people. It is also a region steeped in history, one of the first areas of the New World explored by Christopher Columbus. Central America is both close to the United States and strategically important to it. For nearly a century ships of the U.S. and the world have made good use of the Panama Canal. And for longer than that breakfast tables have been graced by the bananas and other tropical fruits that Central America produces in abundance.

Central America is closer to North America and other peoples of the world with each passing day. Globalized trade brings the region's products to world markets as never before. And there is promise that trade agreements will soon unite all nations of the Americas in a great common market. Meanwhile improved road and air links make it easy for visitors to reach Middle America. Central America's tropical flora and fauna are ever more accessible to foreign visitors having an interest in eco-tourism. Other visitors are drawn to the region's dazzling Pacific Ocean beaches, jewel-like scenery, and bustling towns and cities. And everywhere Central America's wonderful and varied peoples are outgoing and welcoming to foreign visitors.

These eight books are intended to provide complete, up-to-date information on the five countries historians call Central America (Guatemala, El Salvador, Honduras, Nicaragua, Costa Rica), as well as on Panama (technically part of South America) and Belize (technically part of North America). Each volume contains chapters on the land, history, economy, people, and cultures of the countries treated. And each country study is written in an engaging style, employing a vocabulary appropriate to young students.

A fruit vendor with his mobile cart on a street in Granada.

All volumes contain colorful illustrations, maps, and up-to-date boxed information of a statistical character, and each is accompanied by a chronology, a glossary, a bibliography, selected Internet resources, and an index. Students and teachers alike will welcome the many suggestions for individual and class projects and reports contained in each country study, and they will want to prepare the tasty traditional dishes described in each volume's recipe section.

This eight-book series is a timely and useful addition to the literature on Central America. It is designed not just to inform, but also to engage school-aged readers with this important and fascinating part of the Americas.

Let me introduce this series as author Charles J. Shields begins each volume: *¡Hola!* You are discovering Central America!

Nicaragua is located on the Pacific Ring of Fire, a region where volcanic activity and earthquakes are common. (Opposite) San Cristóbal in northwestern Nicaragua is the highest volcano in the country, at 5,725 feet (1,745 m). (Right) A lush valley near Managua, the country's capital and largest city.

1 A Land Rich in Natural Resources

¡HOLA! ARE YOU discovering Nicaragua? It's a land of beaches lapped by sparkling seawater, deep forests, long winding rivers, colonial cities, ancient sites thousands of years old, and a huge freshwater lake—the only lake in the world with sharks in it!

Central America's Largest Country

Nicaragua is bordered on the north by Honduras, on the east by the Caribbean Sea, on the south by Costa Rica, and on the west by the Pacific Ocean. Nicaragua is the largest country of Central America, covering an area of 50,464 sq. miles (129,494 sq. km). Nicaragua's maximum length from north to south is about 275 miles (440 km), and its maximum width from east to west is about 280 miles (450 km). In size, it is a little larger than the state of New York. Lake Nicaragua—the one with sharks in it—is in the

9

southwest. With an area of 3,156 square miles (8,157 sq. km), it is the largest lake in Central America. The country's physical geography divides it into three major zones: Pacific lowlands; the wetter, cooler central highlands, and the Caribbean lowlands.

Pacific Lowlands: Where Most Live

The Pacific lowlands, lakes, and western volcanic mountains of Nicaragua—some of which are active—contain the majority of the country's population, most of its cities, and most of its industry.

Nicaragua is mainly urban. In other words, most people live in towns and cities on the Pacific side of Nicaragua. Managua, the capital, is the largest, most developed city in Nicaragua, with a population of nearly 1 million. There are six freshwater lakes near the city of Managua: Lake Managua; Lake Tiscapa; Lake Asososca, which acts as the city's reservoir of drinking water; Lake Jiloá, which has bitter-tasting water and is a favorite

Words to Understand in this Chapter

cay—a low island or reef of sand or coral.
infertile—inadequate for growing.
resin—a natural substance formed by plant secretions and used chiefly in varnishes, printing inks, plastics, and in medicine.
tectonic—having to do with the plates of the earth's crust, or surface.
terrain—shape of the landscape.
trade wind—a wind blowing almost constantly in one direction.

bathing resort; Lake Masaya, which is prized for its swimming and fishing facilities; and Lake Nejapa, where the sulfur-smelling waters are said to have healing properties. The urban centers of León, Granada, Masaya, and Chinandega are all in the west, too.

Because western Nicaragua is located where two major *tectonic* plates collide, earthquakes and volcanic eruptions happen frequently on the Pacific side. Although fumes and ash from volcanoes have damaged farmland at times, earthquakes have been by far more destructive to life and property. Hundreds of shocks occur each year, some of which cause severe damage. Managua was almost destroyed in 1931 and again in 1972 by earthquakes.

Farming in the Central Highlands

The triangular area known as the central highlands lies northeast and east of the Pacific lowlands. The mountain ranges running through this region include the Cordillera Entre Ríos on the Honduras border; the Cordilleras Isabelia and Dariense in the north-central area; and the Huapí, Amerrique, and Yolaina mountains in the southeast. The mountains are highest in the north. Mogotón Peak, at 7,998 ft (2,438 m) in the Cordillera Entre Ríos, is the highest point in the country.

Forests of oak and pine cover the Pacific-facing slopes of this rugged *terrain*. Protected from Caribbean storms by high ridges, these slopes have attracted farmers since Spanish colonial times, and are now well settled. Deep valleys drain easterly toward the Caribbean Sea. On the eastern slopes, rainforests, nourished by tropical weather from the Caribbean, make farming difficult. The rainforests on the eastern side are home to small communities of Amerindians.

Hot and Humid Lowlands in the East

The hot and humid eastern half of Nicaragua has low, level plains. Among the widest Caribbean lowlands in Central America, these plains average 60 miles (100 km) in width. The soil is generally salt-soaked and *infertile*. The coastline is broken up by river mouths and deltas and large coastal lagoons, as well as by the coral reefs, islands, *cays*, and banks. There are a few towns on the east Caribbean coast—Bluefields and Puerto Cabezas are the largest—but the population on that side of the country is much smaller.

Nicaragua's four principal rivers—the San Juan, Coco, Río Grande de Matagalpa, and Prinzapolka—flow downward from the central highlands, through the Caribbean Lowlands, and empty into the Caribbean Sea.

Nicaragua's Climate

Temperature varies little with the seasons in Nicaragua. The elevation of the land is what makes the difference.

The *tierra caliente*, or the "hot land," is characteristic of the foothills and lowlands from sea level to about 1,000 feet of elevation. Here, daytime temperatures average 80° to 95° F (30° to 35° C), and night temperatures drop to around 70° F (21° C) most of the year. The *tierra templada*, or the "temperate land," is characteristic of most of the central highlands, where elevations range between 1,000 and 2,000 feet (305 to 610 meters). Here, daytime temperatures are mild (70° to 75° F; 21° to 23° C), and nights are cool (50 °

Quick Facts: The Geography of Nicaragua

Location: Middle America, bordering both the Caribbean Sea and the North Pacific Ocean, between Costa Rica and Honduras.

Geographic coordinates: 13'00"N, 85'00"W

Area: (slightly smaller than New York)
total: 129,494 sq. km
land: 120,254 sq. km
water: 9,240 sq. km

borders: Costa Rica, 309 km; Honduras, 922 km; coastline: 910 km.

Terrain: extensive Atlantic coastal plains rising to central interior mountains; narrow Pacific coastal plain interrupted by volcanoes.

Climate: tropical in lowlands, cooler in the highlands.

Elevation extremes:
lowest point: Pacific Ocean 0 m
highest point: Mogotón 2,438 m

Natural resources: gold, silver, copper, tungsten, lead, zinc, timber, fish.

Land use:
arable land: 14.81 percent
permanent crops: 1.82 percent
other: 83.37 percent
Irrigated land: 610 sq. km

Source: CIA World Factbook 2015

F; 10° C). *Tierra fría*, the "cold land," is found only on and near the highest peaks of the central highlands, at elevations above 2,000 feet (610 meters). Daytime averages in this region are around 52° F (11° C), with nighttime lows below 45° F (7° C).

Rainfall, however, does vary greatly in Nicaragua. First, rainfall is seasonal—May through October is the rainy season, and December through April is the driest period. Second, the Caribbean lowlands are the wettest section of Central America, receiving between 8 and 16 feet of rain annually. The western slopes of the central highlands and the Pacific lowlands receive considerably less annual rainfall, being protected from humid Caribbean *trade winds* by the peaks of the central highlands.

During the rainy season, eastern Nicaragua often floods along the upper and middle sections of all major rivers. In addition, destructive tropical storms and hurricanes, particularly from July through October, buffet the coast. The high winds and floods accompanying these storms can cause widespread destruction. Now and then, sudden heavy rains (called *papagayo* storms) follow a cold front and sweep from the north through both eastern and western Nicaragua from November through March.

Plants and Animals in Abundance

Nicaragua is fortunate to have some of the best and most abundant resources in Central America. Its volcanic soil is ideal for growing rich crops. Nicaragua also has the largest forests of commercially valuable trees in Central America, covering one-third of the country. Nicaragua's forests contain valuable cedar, mahogany, and pine timber as well as *quebracho* (axbreaker), *guaiacum* (a type of ironwood), *guapinol* (a tree that yields *resin*), and *medlar* (a tree that produces a crabapple-like fruit).

There is also a fascinating variety of wildlife, such as pumas, jaguars, ocelots, margays, various monkeys, deer, and peccaries. Birds range from eagles to egrets to macaws and pelicans. Reptiles include crocodiles, snakes, turtles, and lizards; and a variety of toads, frogs, fishes, and

This wind farm on the shore of Lake Nicaragua produces electrical power.

mollusks. Unfortunately, there is a brisk business in trapping deer, pumas, monkeys, macaws, and parrots and selling them.

National Parks and Nature Preserves

Thirty-one miles south of the border with Honduras is Cerro Saslaya National Park, an area of over 37,000 acres containing some of the most diverse plant and animal life in Nicaragua. Scientific tours, river trips, observation areas, and other activities are popular among researchers and tourists alike.

The Río Indio Biological Reserve is an enormous world-biosphere reserve covering more than three-quarters of a million acres. It is located at the extreme southeast corner of the Caribbean coast, at the border with Costa Rica near the town of Bluefields. It includes rivers, a seacoast, and lowland plains. A tropical rainforest inside the reserve contains medicinal plants, orchids, deer, monkeys, tapirs, and other mammals, as well as manatees and waterfowl in the marshy areas.

The Miskitos Key National Park is a cluster of 80 coral islands located offshore and slightly to the north of Puerto Cabezas. This marine biological reserve is considered to be one of the loveliest recreational areas in Central America, and is known for its sport fishing and diving.

TEXT-DEPENDENT QUESTIONS

1. In what region of Nicaragua do most people live?
2. What mountain in the Cordillera Entre Ríos is the highest point in Nicaragua?
3. What are Nicaragua's four principal rivers?

In December 1972 a series of earthquakes devastated Managua (opposite), the largest city in Nicaragua. (Right) U.S. President Ronald Reagan poses with Adolfo Calero and other Contra leaders in the White House in August 1987. The scandal that erupted over U.S. support of the Nicaraguan rebels dogged the last years of Reagan's administration.

2 A Troubled History

NICARAGUA'S HISTORY is a troubled one. Since becoming an independent country, the people have suffered from ruthless dictators and repressive governments. In addition, natural disasters such as hurricanes, volcanic eruptions, floods, and earthquakes plague the country.

From Ancient Legends to Conquest

According to Amerindian legend, there are prehistoric footprints near Managua, Nicaragua, left by people fleeing to Lake Managua from a volcanic eruption almost 10,000 years ago. Much later, wanderers found that the soil created by the volcanic ash and minerals was excellent for growing food like beans and corn. As a result, small permanent agricultural communities developed in Nicaragua, although civilization never became as advanced as that of the mighty Aztec and Mayan empires. Nevertheless, the Amerindians of this region were skilled in making stone carvings, pottery, and gold jewelry.

In 1502, Christopher Columbus sighted the coast of the Americas. Twenty years later, the Spanish conquistador Gil González Dávila made the first attempt to gain a foothold in what would become Nicaragua. Although he claimed to have converted some 30,000 natives to Christianity, carried off wagonloads of gold, and discovered a possible water route between the Atlantic and Pacific oceans, González was eventually run out by angry Amerindians. Their leader was a chief named Nicarao, for whom Nicaragua is named. Just two years later, however, in 1524, Spanish colonization began in earnest under Francisco Hernández de Córdoba. Hernandez founded the settlements of Léon and Granada, and Nicaragua became an official part of the Spanish Empire. These two cities still exist today.

Words to Understand in This Chapter

amnesty—the act of an authority (as a government) by which pardon is granted to a large group of individuals.

assassinate—to murder by sudden or secret attack.

civil rights—rights of personal liberty.

destabilize—to make something, particularly a government or economy, unstable.

guerrilla—an irregular armed force.

leftists—those who favor Communist or Socialist ideas.

indigenous—native.

martial—relating to an army or to military life.

trade embargo—a refusal to trade goods and services.

The Spanish conquest was disastrous for the Indians of Nicaragua's Pacific coast. Within three decades, an estimated Indian population of one million plummeted to a few tens of thousands. Half of the *indigenous* people died of Old World diseases, and thousands more were sold into slavery in other New World Spanish colonies.

During the Spanish colonial era, this fort protected Granada from pirate attacks

However, after these crises, the Spanish empire lost interest in Nicaragua, turning its attention to further expansion elsewhere. Granada and León emerged as competing centers of power, although they both suffered from frequent attacks by Caribbean pirates. Late in the 1600s, Great Britain formed an alliance with the Miskito Indians of the Caribbean coastal region, where the trading outpost of Bluefields had been established. The British settled on the Mosquito Coast, as it came to be known, and for a time (1740–86) the region came under British rule.

In the early 19th century, Spanish power went into a rapid decline. As Napoleon's armies marched across Europe, Spain was too deeply involved in war to pay attention to Central America. Its colonies there used the opportunity to break away as independent nations.

Spain officially granted independence to Nicaragua when Guatemala declared independence for all of Central America in 1821.

New Foreign Adventures

After Spain withdrew, Nicaragua lay open to new foreign adventures. The British government strengthened its hold on Bluefields, and in 1848 seized the small Caribbean port of San Juan del Norte, renaming it Greytown.

The discovery of gold in California renewed attention in Nicaragua. American financier Cornelius Vanderbilt began a steamship and carriage operation between Greytown on the Caribbean coast and the Pacific Ocean, making Nicaragua a point of passage between the two oceans long before there was a Panama Canal.

William Walker

The contest between the powerful towns of Léon and Granada continued, however. In 1855, American adventurer William Walker took advantage of the rivalry to capture and loot Granada at the head of a renegade army. He declared himself president and sought statehood from the United States. However, Vanderbilt's transit company supported the Nicaraguans in driving Walker out of the country in 1856, foiling his plans to take over all of Central America, one country at a time.

In 1893, Jose Santos Zelaya led an anti-foreigner revolt that gained him the presidency of Nicaragua and removed the Bluefields region from British control. The United States, predicting that Zelaya would *destabilize* Central America, intervened with U.S. troops to protect American lives and property. With the exception of a brief period in 1925–26, the United States maintained troops in Nicaragua from 1912 until 1933. Beginning in 1927, U.S. marines fought a running battle with rebel forces led by General Augusto Sandino, who wanted the United States out of Nicaragua. The

United States finally withdrew its troops in 1933.

The Somoza Dynasty

The departure of U.S. troops signaled the start of a new round of disorder. National Guard Commander Anastasio Somoza Garcia outmaneuvered his political opponents, including Sandino, who was **assassinated** by National Guard officers, and took over the presidency in 1936. Somoza ruled harshly until his own assassination in 1956. He was succeeded by his son Luis, who shared the presidency with trusted family friends until his death in 1967. Another son, Major General Anastasio Somoza Debayle, became president that year. He continued the Somoza tradition of ruling Nicaragua with an iron fist through the National Guard, relying on the United States for political support, pursuing his political enemies, and amassing an enormous family fortune.

On December 23, 1972, an earthquake leveled the city of Managua, leaving 6,000 dead and 20,000 injured. Somoza declared **martial** law, as if a state of war existed. International aid sent to rebuild Managua found its way into the dictator's hands instead, fueling the anger of his opponents.

Did You Know?

- The national tree of Nicaragua is the *madroño*, which becomes covered in white flowers during the summer. This tree was chosen because of the elegance of its shape and its usefulness.
- The national flower is the *sacuanjoche*, also called the May Flower because that is its flowering month.
- The national bird of Nicaragua is the *guardabarranco*, which lives in the forests of Nicaragua and likes to perch on branches and wave its tail feathers back and forth like a pendulum.

Anastasio Somoza Garcia

A mass uprising ended the Somoza dynasty in 1979. A year earlier, an editor of the anti-Somoza newspaper *La Prensa* had been assassinated. Nicaraguans blamed Somoza. Anti-Somoza **guerrilla** forces under the leadership of the Sandinista National Liberation Front (FSLN)—**leftists** who took their name from General Augusto Sandino—escalated their guerrilla war against the government. The country erupted into civil war. The United States, expecting that a Communist regime would seize power, urged Somoza to resign so that a moderate group could run the country instead. After seven weeks of fighting, Somoza fled the country on July 17, 1979, and the Sandinistas assumed power on July 19.

Contra guerrillas move carefully through the jungle. The war in Nicaragua lasted through most of the 1980s, ending after a peace agreement was signed in 1987.

The Sandinista Era

Although the Sandinistas promised to remain neutral in Central American politics, American president Ronald Reagan accused them of supplying arms to Communist rebels in El Salvador with the aid of Cuba and the Soviet Union. On January 23, 1981, the United States suspended its aid to Nicaragua as a result. The Reagan administration stepped up its opposition to the

Sandinista government by aiding a resistance movement, the Contras, in its efforts to overthrow the Sandinistas.

Elections in Nicaragua on November 4, 1984, resulted in Daniel Ortega, the Sandinista leader, winning the presidency. The United States countered by imposing a **trade embargo** in 1985. Ortega declared a state of national emergency and suspended all **civil rights**. The war between the Sandinistas and the Contras intensified from 1985 to 1987. In the United States, a political scandal occurred when it was discovered that the Reagan administration had secretly supplied weapons and money to the Contras. Because the funds for the Contras came from the illegal sale of weapons to Iran, the scandal became known as the Iran-Contra affair.

Negotiations sponsored by Latin American nations failed to end the war in Nicaragua. However, Oscar Arias Sánchez, president of Costa Rica, proposed a peace plan that succeeded. Five Central American presidents signed Sánchez's peace plan in Guatemala City in 1987, an accomplishment for which he received the Nobel Peace Prize.

The Sandinista government agreed to nationwide elections in February 1990. In these elections, which were proclaimed fair by international observers, Nicaraguan voters elected as their president the candidate of the National Opposition Union, Violeta Barrios de Chamorro, the widow of slain *La Prensa* newspaper editor Pedro Joaquín Chamorro.

A Democratic Transfer of Power

Violeta Barrios de Chamorro sought to lead the country to peace and prosperity, and to safeguard human rights and property, but 11 years of war had left its mark. Corruption was widespread, and the business community became impatient with the slow pace of change. Former Managua mayor Arnoldo Alemán won the 1996 presidential election. More than 76 percent of Nicaragua's 2.4 million eligible voters participated. The next highest vote getter was Daniel Ortega, the former president and Sandinista leader. The first transfer of power in recent Nicaraguan history from one democratically elected president to another took place on January 10, 1997, when the Alemán government was inaugurated.

In 1998, Hurricane Mitch devastated the country, killing more than 9,000 people, leaving two million people homeless, and causing $10 billion in damages. Many Nicaraguans fled to the United States under an immigration *amnesty* program extended from the Sandinista era.

In 2001, conservative businessman Enrique Bolanos was elected president, defeating the Sandinista candidate Ortega. However, in 2006 Ortega won the presidency, returning to power in Nicaragua after a 16-year absence. As president, Ortega continued to have a tense relationship with the United States. He established closer ties with other nations that often opposed U.S. policies, including Iran, Cuba, and Venezuela.

In 2007, Hurricane Felix devastated the northern Caribbean coast of Nicaragua. The powerful storm destroyed about 9,000 homes and killed 130 people in the country. Many countries, including the United States, sent aid to help those who had been displaced by the disaster.

In 2011, Daniel Ortega was re-elected president by a comfortable margin, receiving 62 percent of the vote. Under his leadership, a $50 billion plan to build a huge shipping canal across Nicaragua was approved. When completed, the Nicaragua Grand Canal, as it is known, would be wider than the Panama Canal, allowing the largest cargo ships and oil tankers to pass through. However, environmentalists have complained that the project would cause terrible pollution in Lake Nicaragua, which is the source of drinking water for most of the people. A company called the Hong Kong Nicaragua Canal Development

Sandinista leader Daniel Ortega returned to power in 2006, and has ruled the country as president since that time.

Investment Company received a lease to build and manage the canal. Work began on the project in early 2015.

In January of 2014, Nicaragua's National Assembly approved a change to the constitution that eliminated the limit on presidential terms. This change would permit Ortega to run for a third term in the 2016 election.

TEXT-DEPENDENT QUESTIONS

1. What two Spanish settlements did Francisco Hernández de Córdoba establish in 1524?
2. What National Opposition Union candidate was elected president in 1991?
3. What change was made to Nicaragua's constitution in 2014? Why was this change made?

(Right) Banana plants grow on a farm in Nicaragua. Agriculture is the most important sector of the country's economy, and the way in which most people make their living. (Opposite) The enormous statue Jesus of the Mercy watches over the fishing boats in the harbor of San Juan del Sur, on Nicaragua's Pacific coast.

3 A Weak Economy

NICARAGUA IS THE LEAST-DEVELOPED COUNTRY in Central America. It is also one of the poorest countries in the entire Western Hemisphere, behind only Haiti. According to recent date, more than 40 percent of Nicaraguans lives below the poverty line.

However, in recent years there have been positive economic signs. The Nicaraguan economy has been growing about 5 percent a year—a faster rate of growth than many other Central American countries. Unemployment, once widespread, has fallen throughout the country. And the national rate of **inflation** has dropped significantly, although it is still rather high at about 6 percent in 2014.

Part of the reason for Nicaragua's economic growth is an increase in trade with other nations. In 2007, Nicaragua signed a major trade agreement with the United States and several other countries in Central America

27

and the Caribbean. The purpose of the Central American-Dominican Republic Free Trade Agreement (CAFTA-DR) is to make it easier for business in the participating countries—which also include El Salvador, Guatemala, Honduras, Costa Rica, and the Dominican Republic—to work together by eliminating tariffs, or taxes on certain goods.

Despite the increase in jobs that economic growth brings, many Nicaraguans must move to other countries, such as Costa Rica or the United States, to find work. **Remittances**, or money that these workers send home to their families each month, represents a significant source of income. There are approximately 1 million Nicaraguans working in other countries, and they send home a total of more than $400 million annually.

Nicaragua does receive **foreign aid** from the United States, as well as from international organizations like the International Monetary Fund (IMF) and the World Bank. However, as a condition of lending money these groups have insisted that Nicaragua take steps to reduce poverty, maintain fair government, and guarantee respect for human rights.

Words to Understand in this Chapter

domestic—relating to the internal affairs of a nation or country.
foreign aid—financial assistance given by one country to another.
inflation—when the purchasing power of money drops.
remittances—an amount of money, often sent by mail or by bank transfer, from a
    foreign worker to family members in his or her native country.

Agriculture

About two-fifths of Nicaragua's workers are engaged in agriculture, forestry, and fishing, which produce about one-fourth of the total national income. Today, Nicaragua's main export products include coffee, seafood, beef, and sugar. Crops grown by farmers for their own use include corn, beans, rice, sorghum, plantains, and cassava. Other homegrown fruits and vegetables are also raised by Nicaraguans for their own tables. Cattle are a major a source of hides, meat, and dairy products. Other livestock include goats, hogs, horses, and sheep.

Shrimping is the most important fishing activity in Nicaragua, with most of the catch from the Pacific and Caribbean coasts being sold for export. Lobsters also are exported, but in smaller amounts. Like

Seedlings on a coffee plantation in Nicaragua. Coffee is one of the country's main exports.

Nicaragua's forests, the country's fisheries have not become as commercial as they could be, mainly because of lack of investment. Most fishing takes place by families feeding themselves.

Investment in Industry and Tourism

Nicaragua's industry has been based on producing consumer products—goods to be purchased in stores. But to manufacture them, local businesses must rely heavily on raw material imports. Since the late 1990s, the government has supported creating a greater variety of products using *domestic* raw materials found in Nicaragua. Some of these new products made inside Nicaragua's borders include refined petroleum, matches, footwear, soap and vegetable oils, cement, alcoholic beverages, and textiles.

The Corn Islands, off the coast of Nicaragua, are attractive to tourists who want to visit an undeveloped Caribbean island.

Quick Facts: The Economy of Nicaragua

Gross Domestic Product (GDP*): $27.97 billion

GDP per capita: $4,500

Natural resources: gold, silver, copper, tungsten, lead, zinc, timber, fish.

Industry (26 percent of GDP): food processing, chemicals, machinery and metal products, knit and woven apparel, petroleum refining and distribution, beverages, footwear, wood, electric wire harness manufacturing, mining.

Agriculture (17 percent of GDP): coffee, bananas, sugarcane, rice, corn, tobacco, sesame, soya, beans; beef, veal, pork, poultry, dairy products; shrimp, lobsters, cotton.

Services (58 percent of GDP): tourism, government, other.

Annual Exports: $2.4 billion—coffee, beef, gold, sugar, peanuts, shrimp and lobster, tobacco, cigars, automobile wiring harnesses, textiles, apparel, cotton.

Annual Imports: $5.65 billion—consumer goods, machinery and equipment, raw materials, petroleum products.

Unemployment rate: 7.2 percent

Economic growth rate: 4.6 percent

Currency exchange rate: 26.84 Nicaraguan cordobas = U.S. $1 (2015).

* GDP or gross domestic product—the total value of goods and services produced in a year.
Sources: CIA World Factbook 2015; Bloomberg.com. All figures 2014 estimates, unless otherwise noted.

Of all the country's minerals, only gold has been mined intensively. Mineral reserves in Nicaragua, of which there are many, have not been mined very much because of lack of investment. That is beginning to change thanks to CAFTA-DR.

Tourism has become the second-largest industry in the nation, and has poured much-needed money into the Nicaraguan economy. In 2010, the country surpassed 1 million foreign visitors for the first time ever. Nicaragua's ecological attractions—beaches, volcanoes, and wildlife—hold

Nicaragua's currency is called the cór-doba. The bills feature pictures of famous Nicaraguans on one side, with scenery on the other.

the potential to draw many more tourists in the future. The Corn Islands, which are located located about 44 miles (70 km) off the Caribbean coast of Nicaragua, have become a popular destination.

A Limited Transportation System

Most of Nicaragua's transportation system is limited to the Pacific lowlands, where the major cities are located. There is a network of highways, but during the rainy season, roads sometimes wash out. Nicaragua's highway system includes a 255-mile (410 km) section of the Pan-American Highway, which runs through the west from Honduras to Costa Rica. Another major road runs from the Pan-American Highway, 24 miles (39 km) from Managua eastward, to Port Esperanza at Rama. A third connects Managua with Puerto Cabezas on the Caribbean.

Railways in Nicaragua total just a few hundred miles. The main line runs from Granada, northwest to Corinto, on the Pacific Ocean. A branch line leads north from León to the coffee area of Carazo.

Ocean ports provide Nicaragua with important trading links to other countries. The chief ocean ports of Corinto, which handles most foreign trade, Puerto Sandino, and San Juan del Sur serve the Pacific coastal area.

The ports on the Caribbean side include Puerto Cabezas and Bluefields. The short rivers in the west can be navigated by small craft. In the east, the Coco River is navigable at its lower end for medium-sized vessels.

Nicaragua has two major airports. The main international airport, seven miles from Managua, has service to North America and Latin America. Another large commercial airport is located at Puerto Cabezas. Other airports have scheduled domestic flights.

The Nicaraguan Grand Canal, which would cut across the country to create a shipping lane between the Atlantic and Pacific oceans, would provide significant revenue to the country. Work on this project began in 2015.

 TEXT-DEPENDENT QUESTIONS

1. What sector of Nicaragua's economy employs the most people?
2. What Caribbean islands have become popular among tourists.
3. What are the five major ports of Nicaragua?

(Opposite) Laguna de Apoyeque is a large lake that formed in a caldera, or volcanic depression, near the city of Managua. It is 1.7 miles (2.8 km) wide and 1,300 feet (400 m) deep. (Right) A crowd celebrates Independence Day, September 15, in the plaza in Granada.

4 A People With Divided Views of Their Country

HISTORICALLY, THE SETTLEMENT of Nicaragua has been uneven across the country. In *pre-Columbian* times, the Pacific lowlands, with its fertile soils and relatively mild climate, supported a large, dense Amerindian population. The forested central highlands held smaller numbers of people. And the hot, muggy Caribbean lowlands were only sparsely populated.

Since the Spanish conquest in the early 1500s, Nicaragua's basic settlement pattern has largely remained unchanged. More than 60 percent of Nicaraguans live within the narrow strip of the Pacific lowlands. About 30 percent live in the central highlands. And the Caribbean lowlands, covering more than half of the national territory, holds less than 10 percent of the population.

Most Nicaraguans identify themselves as *mestizos*—people of mixed European and Amerindian descent who share a national Hispanic culture.

35

Until the 19th century, there was still a large Native American minority in Nicaragua. Gradually, however, most Amerindians have been *assimilated* into the mainstream culture. Today, the country's racial composition is roughly as follows: *mestizo*, 69 percent; European, 17 percent; Amerindian, 5 percent; and Creoles or people of predominately African ancestry, 9 percent.

Nicaragua has been spared the bitter conflict between whites, *mestizos*, and Amerindians that has torn apart other Latin American countries. However, differences in culture, language, and appearance create friction between *mestizos* of the central highlands and Pacific lowlands and non-*mestizo* minorities of the east or Caribbean lowlands.

West/East Friction

The most widely spoken language in Nicaragua is Spanish, except in the Caribbean lowlands, where a mix of English, Spanish, and native Indian is

Words to Understand in This Chapter

assimilate—to integrate somebody into a larger group, so that differences are minimized or eliminated; cultural blending.
barrio—a ghetto, or ethnic communities.
compulsory—something that is required by law; mandatory.
convert—someone who has changed religious beliefs.
Pre-Columbian—a term referring to the period of American history before the arrival of Christopher Columbus at the end of the 15th century.
rural—in the countryside.
shantytowns—villages made of shacks.

spoken. More than language, however, separates the East and West coasts. The west, where the major urban centers are located, is populated by Spanish-speaking whites and *mestizos*, both of whom regard themselves as Nicaraguans and participate in its national life of politics, the arts, athletics, and so on. In addition to speaking Spanish, many professional people on the west coast—those in business, government, education, and science— also speak English.

Almost no pockets of separate Amerindian culture remain in the western half of the country. Indian languages on the west coast have disappeared, even though their influence remains in place-names and many nouns in Nicaraguan Spanish. Nicaraguans sometimes make mention of the "Indian" **barrios** of Monimbó Amerindians in Masaya, of Subtiava

Two Miskito children eat sugar cane in their home in Tasbapauni, a tiny village on the banks of the Prinzapolka River in Nicaragua's Caribbean region. The Miskito are one of three Amerindian tribes native to the region; the others are the Sumo and Rama.

Amerindians in León, and to almost-mainstream Matagalpan Amerindians in the central highlands. However, the ways these groups live make them almost identical with *mestizos*.

In the eastern half of Nicaragua, far away from the decision-making centers of power on the other side of the mountains, Amerindians and Creoles prefer to remain apart in language, customs, and lifestyles.

The eastern side of Nicaragua is more diverse than the western side. Even though Spanish-speaking *mestizos* are the largest single group on the east coast also, the population of that region also includes Miskito, Sumo, and Rama Indians, as well as Black Caribs—also known as Garifuna, the descendants of African slaves and Carib Indians—and Creoles, or English-speaking blacks. The Amerindians of the eastern half of the country remain ethnically separate and still use tribal customs and languages. Many live in small communities in the rainforest on the eastern slopes of the Central highlands.

In the mid-1980s, the Sandinista government divided the eastern side of Nicaragua into two separate regions and granted the people limited self-rule. Under the 1987 constitution and the Atlantic Coast Autonomy Law enacted the same year, Miskito, Sumo, Rama, and Creole-English were given equal rank in public life with Spanish. Constitutional reform in 1995 further guaranteed that the region's unique cultures would be respected and gave the inhabitants a voice in how the area's natural resources would be used.

These measures gave peoples on the east coast greater self-determination. But in another way, they were also an official way of saying that the interests of the non-*mestizo* population are different from most of the rest of Nicaragua.

Quick Facts: The People of Nicaragua

Population: 5,848,641

Ethnic groups: mestizo (mixed Amerindian and white) 69%; white 17%; black 9%; Amerindian 5%.

Age structure:
0–14 years: 29.3 percent
15–64 years: 66 percent
65 years and over: 4.7 percent

Population growth rate: 1.02 percent

Birth rate: 18.41 births/1,000 population

Death rate: 5.07 deaths/1,000 population

Infant mortality rate: 20.36 deaths/1,000 live births

Life expectancy at birth:
total population: 72.72 years
male: 70.57 years
female: 74.98 years

Total fertility rate: 1.99 children born per woman

Religions: Roman Catholic 58.5%; Protestant 23.2% (Evangelical 21.6%, Moravian 1.6%); Jehovah's Witnesses 0.9%; other 1.6%; none 15.7% (2005 est.).

Languages: Spanish (official); Miskito 2.2%; other 2.5% (2005 est.).

Literacy: 78% percent (2005 est.)

Source: CIA World Factbook 2015. All figures 2014 estimates, unless otherwise noted.

Religion and Education

There is no official religion in Nicaragua, but a majority of the people practice Roman Catholicism. In recent decades, Protestant Christian denominations have gained hundreds of thousands of *converts*, owing to missionary work and preaching by Christian fundamentalists. Very small Jewish communities can be found in Nicaragua's larger cities, and the Jehovah's Witnesses, a Christian sect, has made some inroads as well.

Schooling in Nicaragua in the primary and secondary grades is free and *compulsory*. However, many children cannot attend because there no local

Did You Know?

- Nicaragua has a republic-type government which consists of executive, legislative, and judicial branches. The current constitution was adopted in 1987, and has been amended numerous times, most recently in 2014.
- The president and vice president are elected on the same ticket by popular vote for a five-year term; in 2011, Daniel Ortega Saavedra was re-elected president of Nicaragua.
- There are 92 seats in Nicaragua's National Assembly. 90 members are elected by the people to serve five-year terms). The previous president and the runner-up in the last presidential election have the other two seats in the Assembly.
- The Supreme Court, or *Corte Suprema*, consists of 16 judges elected for seven-year terms by the National Assembly.
- Major political parties in Nicaragua include the Sandinista National Liberation Front (FSLN), the Independent Liberal Party (PLI), and the Liberal Constitutionalist Party (PLC)
- The capital of Nicaragua is Managua.

schools, especially in *rural* areas. Also, children are expected to help their families at an early age, even if that means getting a full-time job. Most drop out long before high school. Only about 20 percent of children who start school reach high school. There are universities in Nicaragua, which have been attracting an increasing number of students in recent years. The literacy rate in Nicaragua—the percentage of the population older than 15 who can read and write—is about 78 percent, which is comparable to other Central American countries.

A Slowly Growing Population

From the 1950s to the 2000s, Nicaragua experienced a population boom, due to a combination of a high birth rate and rapid urban growth. The population quadrupled between 1965 and 2000, growing a much raster rate than the rest of Central America. Families of six to eight children were not uncommon in Nicaragua. However, due to poverty and disease people did not live very long.

The average life expectancy of a Nicaraguan in the 1950s was just 45 years

Since 2000, Nicaragua has increased the average life expectancy of its residents to around 72 years, which is about the world average. This improvement is largely due to increased access to clean drinking water, better sanitation, and improved health care and immunization of children against infectious diseases. However, the population growth rate has slowed significantly, to around 1 percent a year by 2015. Nicaraguan women are having fewer children, and smaller families have become more common in the country.

One area of concern is that there is a high birth rate among adolescent Nicaraguans, especially in the rural areas of the country. Experts note that this issue tends to perpetuate a cycle of poverty and low educational attainment in this region.

People swim in Lake Nicaragua. The proposed Grand Canal project has raised all sort of environmental concerns related to the pollution of Central America's largest freshwater lake.

Children attend classes at the Las Torres elementary school in Managua. Although education is free in Nicaragua, there are few schools, especially in rural areas. Many children drop out before reaching high school.

Another thing that slows Nicaragua's population growth is emigration to other countries. For more than a century, Nicaraguan men have migrated to Costa Rica, where they can find jobs harvesting bananas, coffee, and other labor-intensive crops during the harvesting season. Political turmoil and natural disasters have also caused Nicaraguans to emigrate. Today there are more than 300,000 Nicaraguans living in Costa Rica, many of them illegally. In recent years, the issue of illegal immigration has led to tensions between Costa Rica and Nicaragua.

An Urban Society

The growth in Nicaragua's population has mostly come in the cities. Today, more than two-third of Nicaraguans live in urban areas, mostly around Lake

Nicaragua. According to the country's most recent census, Managua's population is more than 1 million. This figure does not include the large number of people who live in **shantytowns** around the city. No other Nicaraguan city is anywhere near that size.

The country's second-largest city is León, with a population of roughly 200,000. The other important cities include Matagalpa (pop. 167,000), Masaya (pop. 151,000), Chinandega (pop. 134,000), and Granada (pop. 124,000). Somewhat smaller are the principal towns on the Caribbean coast: Bluefields and Puerto Cabezas.

 TEXT-DEPENDENT QUESTIONS

1. What are the two regions of Nicaragua? Why is there friction between them?
2. Why has the average lifespan of Nicaraguan residents improved over the last decade?
3. What is Nicaragua's second-largest city?

(Opposite) Heavy traffic and pedestrians crows the streets in a busy market in Granada. (Right) Small fishing boats line the beach in front of modest shacks.

5 An Identity Still Evolving

WITH A POPULATION of nearly six million people and a history created from the overlap between an Amerindian and European past, Nicaragua offers an uneven mix of culture and tradition. The majority of Nicaraguans, including *mestizos*, whites and blacks, share a Hispanic culture. On the Caribbean coast, non-Spanish speaking and non-Catholic people prefer a blend of English and native culture. The Sandinista revolution of 1979 and the civil war of the 1980s shook the foundation of the entire country, however, leaving many Nicaraguans wondering what their national identity will be in the future.

The majority of Nicaraguans—those who live on the Pacific coast—have developed their culture from a mixture of the native Indians and the Spanish settlers of the 16th century. Consequently, many of the cities retain a strong Spanish influence, and Catholicism is the most widely practiced religion.

The Caribbean coast, on the other hand, was more influenced by the English who controlled that region until the 19th century. Blacks and native peoples—Miskito, Rama, and Sumu—preferred to deal with the British rather than the Spanish and adapted some of their ways. For example, in the southeastern town of Bluefields, where many blacks live who are descended from slaves, the annual celebration of *Mayo Ya* combines English Maypole dancing with Caribbean folklore and African music and dance. Bluefields is also home to reggae music. Added to this, Protestant religions are more common here than on the Pacific coast, although Catholicism is still the dominant religion. Outside of this interesting mix of culture and tradition, some Amerindians living in this region prefer to remain largely non-Western in their ways altogether.

The Catholic Heritage

The majority of Nicaraguans are Catholic, and most communities observe a religious calendar dotted with festive parades honoring the local patron saint. Each city in Nicaragua has its own patron saint, and some saints are shared between towns. Devout people offer gifts to saints in exchange for

Words to Understand in this Chapter

excavate—to dig out and remove.
imperialist—one country extending power over another.

blessings, such as healing, a good crop, or children. Part of the tradition of honoring a saint is holding a fiesta, too.

Fiestas are holidays of fun and excitement in villages, towns, and cities. A statue of the saint being honored is carried through the streets, signaling the start of traditional dances, plays, or rituals. Following the saint's images, people offer flower arrangements, and they pay their "promises" with little gold and silver objects and fruit bunches. As night falls, exploding firecrackers and fireworks add to the pleasure of entertainment by roving musicians, performing clowns, and speeches by local leaders.

Literature: a National Passion

Literature is one of Nicaragua's most popular arts. Works by Rubén Darío (1867–1916), known as the "prince of Spanish-American poetry," and recent works by Nicaraguan poets, fiction writers, and essayists can be found in most bookshops. Although Darío spent much time outside Nicaragua, he wrote often about the conflicting beauties of his homeland.

Even in literature, however, issues of race, class, and national identity divide Nicaraguans. To some, the works of Darío are examples of literature aimed at the professional class of better-educated people. The revolutionary period from the late 1970s through 1990 produced another kind of artistic expression. Unlike the Somoza regime, which had valued traditional 19th-century Western culture, the Sandinistas supported what they termed "democratizing, national, anti-*imperialist*" art forms, both professional and amateur.

Today, Nicaragua's museums and libraries are small and poorly maintained. The National Library and the National Museum in Managua, as

Did You Know?

These are the official holidays in Nicaragua. Other occasions are celebrated with parties and carnivals or family get-togethers. In addition, many towns hold a *festejo*, or festival, to honor its patron saint.

- January 1—New Year's Day
- May 1—Labor Day
- May 30—Mothers' Day
- July 19—National Liberation Day
- August 1—Fiesta Day
- September 14—San Jacinto Fight Day
- September 15—Independence Day
- November 2—All Souls Day
- December 8—Feast of the Immaculate Conception
- December 25—Christmas Day

well as the Rubén Darío museum in Ciudad Darío, are in poor condition.

On the other hand, folk traditions in Nicaragua continue to be strong and expressed in arts and crafts, popular religious ceremonies, and country songs (*corridos*). Many Nicaraguan folktales involve magic cures and evil spells. Some of the eeriest come from the people of Ometepe, an island in Lake Nicaragua with two volcanoes. These teach respect for nature and show how humans sometimes mistreat each other.

Architecture from Long Ago

Earthquakes and war have destroyed much of Nicaragua's colonial architecture, though some still remains. Many of Nicaragua's landmark buildings are in Granada and León, the two cities that have long served as the country's military, cultural, and religious centers.

Fine examples of colonial architecture in Granada begin with La Merced Church, the construction of which began in 1543. The main Cathedral of Granada makes up one side of the central plaza, as cathedrals do in all Spanish colonial cities. Xalteva Church, and the walls that surround its neighborhood, date to the early 17th century.

The original city of León, at the foot of the Momotombo volcano, was destroyed by an earthquake in 1609, but the ruins have been ***excavated***. In the resettled city of León, the Metropolitan Cathedral represents massive religious architecture from the mid-18th century and is the largest cathedral in Central America. This cathedral not only houses artistic

The cathedral of León is a fine example of colonial-era architecture.

In a parade in Managua, children wear masks to represent Spanish visitors to Nicaragua. The parade is part of the country's October 12 celebration of Columbus Day, marking the date of the explorer's arrival in the New World.

masterpieces, it is also the final resting place of the country's most prestigious figures, including the poet Rubén Darío, who is buried at the foot of a statue of St. Paul and guarded by a sorrowful lion.

Food, Drink, and Music

The Nicaraguan food, like many dishes in Central American, is based on corn. Corn has a deep cultural meaning. Quetzalcoatl, a mythical hero who guided the Amerindians, put a grain of corn on the lips of the first man and woman, enabling them to think and work. Today, corn is the main ingredient used in many dishes, drinks, desserts, and other refreshments. Cassava (yucca), beans, and chili peppers are also widely used as ingredients in different Nicaraguan dishes.

A typical meal in Nicaragua consists of eggs or meat, beans and rice, salad (cabbage and tomatoes), tortillas, and fruit in season. Food is usually scooped up in tortillas instead of using knives and forks. Most common of all Nicaraguan foods is *gallo pinto*, a blend of rice and beans. Other traditional dishes include *bajo* (a mix of beef, green and ripe plantains, and cassava) and *vigorón* (cassava served with fried pork skins and coleslaw). Street vendors sell drinks such as *tiste*, made from cacao and corn, and *posol con leche*, a corn-and-milk drink. Roasted corn on the cob is also sold on the streets. Restaurants, particularly in Managua, serve a variety of foods, including Spanish, Italian, French, Latin American, and Chinese.

The marimba is the national instrument. It is constructed from hard-wood plates, placed over bamboo or metal tubes of different lengths. The tubes are played using two soft hammers, like a xylophone. The marimba blends well with guitars and percussion instruments.

During festival times, people look forward to seeing traditional dances and skits performed to music. The most popular are "Los Caballeros Elegantes del Toro Huaco" (The Elegant Knights of the Huaco Bull), "La Burla del Güegüense" (The Güegüense Trick), and "El Drama Épico del Gigante" (The Amazing Story of the Giants).

TEXT-DEPENDENT QUESTIONS

1. What are some example of colonial-era architecture in Nicaragua?
2. What Nicaraguan instrument is made from hardwood and bamboo?

Recipes

Fresco de Piña y Arroz (Pineapple and Rice Drink)

(Makes 6 to 8 cups)
16-oz. can of sliced pineapple
1/2 cup rice
strainer
sugar

Directions:

1. Place drained pineapple slices in a pot. Add enough water to cover by about two inches.
2. Bring to a boil for about 10 minutes, and then add about 1/2 cup of uncooked white rice. Keep boiling until the rice splits or puffs.
3. Let cool. Strain out the liquid.
4. Add about twice as much water as you got from the pot. Add sugar to taste. Drink very cold.

Picos

(Serves about 12)
Refrigerated biscuit dough
Brown sugar
Quajada—a soft cheese from Nicaragua (you can use farmer's cheese instead)

Directions:

1. Roll the bread dough thin, and cut into large triangles.
2. Place about half a teaspoon of brown sugar and a small piece of cheese in the center of the triangle. Fold over the other corners of the triangle and overlap them in the center.
3. Bake until the bread is browned.

Tres Leches (Three Milks)—a cake

(Makes one 12" x 8" cake)
5 eggs
1 cup white sugar
1 cup self-rising flour
1 teaspoon vanilla extract
1 small can sweetened condensed milk
1 small can evaporated milk
1/2 cup milk
1 tablespoon vanilla extract
3 egg whites
1 cup white sugar
1 tablespoon vanilla extract

Directions:

1. Grease and flour an 8 x 12 inch pan. Preheat the oven to 350° F.
2. Separate the 5 eggs, and beat the egg whites in a large mixing bowl. Add the cup of sugar slowly to the egg whites, beating constantly. Add the yolks one by one, beating well after each addition. Stir in the teaspoon of vanilla.
3. Sift the flour, and stir it into the egg mixture.
4. Pour the batter into the prepared pan. Bake the cake for 20 minutes or until done. Cool.
5. Blend the sweetened condensed milk, evaporated milk, milk, and a tablespoon of vanilla. Pour over the cooled cake. (The cake is meant to be a little soggy. Keep it refrigerated.)
To make meringue frosting: Beat 3 egg whites to soft peaks. Gradually add 1 cup sugar, and beat until stiff peaks form. Stir in 1 teaspoon vanilla. Frost the cake.

Chocolate Bananas

(Makes 16)
8 firm bananas (not too ripe)
2 small cans of chocolate syrup
16 Popsicle sticks
A knife
Wax paper

Directions:
1. Peel bananas and cut in half.
2. Stick a Popsicle stick into each banana, making sure it goes in straight.
3. Coat the bananas with chocolate syrup by dipping them into a tall glass filed with the syrup.
4. Place the bananas on wax paper over a plate or cookie sheet, and put the bananas into a freezer until frozen.

Gallo Pinto (Speckled Rooster)

(This dish gets its name from the appearance of the mixture. It does not actually contain rooster or any other type of meat. Serves 12)
2 tablespoons of oil
1/2 cup chopped onions
1 teaspoon red chili powder
8 12-oz. cans of pinto beans
2 cups cooked white rice

Directions:
1. Heat oil in a large skillet (don't let it smoke).
2. Add chili powder and onions. Fry until the onions are golden.
3. Mix equal portions of cooked red beans and cooked white rice, and stir-fry in oil until tender. The rice should be a little brown.

Series Glossary

Amerindian—a term for the indigenous peoples of North, Central, and South America before the arrival of Europeans in the late 15th century.

civil liberty—the right of people to do or say things that are not illegal without being stopped or interrupted by the government.

conquistador—any one of the Spanish leaders of the conquest of the Americas in the 1500s.

Communism—a political system in which all resources, industries, and property are considered to be held in common by all the people, with government as the central authority responsible for controlling all economic and social activity.

coup d'état—the violent overthrow of an existing government by a small group.

criollo—a resident of Spain's New World colonies who was born in North America to parents of Spanish ancestry. During the colonial period, criollos ranked above mestizos in the social order.

deforestation—the action or process of clearing forests.

economic system—the production, distribution, and consumption of goods and services within a country.

ecotourism—a form of tourism in which resorts attempt to minimize the impact of visitors on the local environment, contribute to conserving habitats, and employ local people.

embargo—a government restriction or restraint on commerce, especially an order that prohibits trade with a particular nation.

exploit—to take advantage of something; to use something unfairly.

foreign aid—financial assistance given by one country to another.

free trade—trade based on the unrestricted exchange of goods, with tariffs (taxes) only used to create revenue, not keep out foreign goods.

Mesoamerica—the region of southern North America that was inhabited before the arrival of the Spaniards.

mestizo—a person of mixed Amerindian and European (typically Spanish) descent.

plaza—the central open square at the center of colonial-era cities in Latin America.

plebiscite—a vote by which the people of an entire country express their opinion on a particular government or national policy.

population density—a measurement of the number of people living in a specific area, such a square mile or square kilometer.

pre-Columbian—referring to a time before the 1490s, when Christopher Columbus landed in the Americas.

regime—a period of rule by a particular government, especially one that is considered to be oppressive.

service industry—any business, organization, or profession that does work for a customer, but is not involved in manufacturing.

Create a map of Nicaragua's west

Make a layered map by using several transparency sheets. On one, draw the natural features of Nicaragua; on a second, place the major cities and towns; on a third, show the highways, rail lines, and airports. Place each one on top of the other on a transparency projector to show classmates how Nicaragua is "tilted toward the west" in terms of its population and development.

Create a "climate map" of Nicaragua

Using transparencies, show the three lands of Nicaragua—the hot land, the mild land, and the cold land.

Create a map of Nicaragua's food resources

Using this book, an encyclopedia, and the Internet as resources, find out the areas where important fruits, trees, and vegetables of Nicaragua are grown. Draw a map of the country, pointing out which foods are grown in which regions. You could also show where fishing takes place.

Flashcards

Using the glossary in this book, create flashcards. Put the term on one side and the definition on the other. Practice with the cards in pairs. Then, choose two teams of three. Select a referee to say the term out loud, and then call on someone to give the definition. The referee's decision is final. Award points for each correct answer. You can also read the definition, and ask for the correct term instead!

Presentations

- Memorize and recite two poems by Rubén Darío (you can find translations on the Internet).
- Find three pieces of marimba music, and play them for the class. Explain each title. (Your local reference librarian can help you.)

- There are letters on the Internet written by American students studying abroad in Nicaragua. Find one and read it aloud to the class. Does it give you any insights into the country?

Reports

Write one-page, five-paragraph reports answering any of the following questions. Begin with a paragraph of introduction, then three paragraphs each developing one main idea, followed by a conclusion that summarizes your topic:

- Why are there sharks in Lake Nicaragua.
- Who were the Caribbean pirates and how did they live?
- What was the Iran-Contra Affair? What was the result?
- Who built the Pan-American Highway? Where does it go?
- What is the International Monetary Fund? Where does it get its money? What does it do?
- Draw pictures and provide one-paragraph descriptions of any five animals of Nicaragua mentioned in Chapter One, "A Land Rich in Natural Resources."

Write one-page biographies of any one of these people:

Francisco Hernández de Córdoba	Cornelius Vanderbilt	William Walker
General Augusto Sandino	Anastasio Somoza Debayle	Daniel Ortega
Oscar Arias Sánchez	Rubén Darío	

1509	Spanish settlers arrive in Panama; by 1524, the Spanish have moved into the rest of Central America.
1821	Central American provinces proclaim independence from Spain.
1855	American mercenary William Walker is hired by a Nicaraguan political party to topple the president; he takes control of the government and sets himself up as president; he is ousted the next year.
1909	Dictator Jose Santos Zelaya is overthrown in Nicaragua; chaos and instability follow, leading to U.S. financial and military intervention.
1927	Potential peace accord among fighting factions in Nicaragua provides basis for U.S. occupation and subsequent elections; General Augusto C. Sandino leads a guerrilla force against the U.S. Marines.
1931	An earthquake destroys most of the capital city, Managua.
1933	General Anastasio Somoza Garcia is named director of the new National Guard in Nicaragua; the U.S. Marines withdraw.
1956	Anastasio Somoza is assassinated; his sons, Luis and Anastasio Jr., retain control of Nicaragua.
1961	The Sandinista National Liberation Front (FSLN) is founded in Nicaragua.
1967	Anastasio Somoza Debayle is "elected" president of Nicaragua.
1972	An earthquake devastates Managua; Somoza's mishandling of crisis and of international relief funds increases anger toward the regime.
1979	Somoza is overthrown, and a new governing coalition dominated by the Sandinistas assumes power.
1981	The U.S. halts aid to Nicaragua after finding evidence that Nicaragua, Cuba, and the Soviet Union are supplying arms to rebels in El Salvador.

1984	Daniel Ortega, leader of the FSLN, is "elected" president of Nicaragua.
1986	The U.S. government admits that the Reagan administration provided military aid to the Contras, using funds diverted from the sale of weapons to Iran. The covert operation becomes known as the Iran-Contra Affair.
1988	The Sandinistas and Contras begin a cease-fire and are parties to a peace plan developed by Oscar Arias Sánchez of Costa Rica.
1990	Violeta Barrios de Chamorro of the UNO party (National Opposition Union) defeats the FSLN's Daniel Ortega in internationally observed presidential elections; Sandinistas and Contras sign a permanent cease-fire.
1997	Arnoldo Alemán is inaugurated as president, thus completing the first democratic and peaceful transfer of the presidency in Nicaragua's history.
2001	Ortega is defeated in fall presidential election by Enrique Bolanos.
2006	Ortega is elected president; the Nicaraguan government signs the Central American Free Trade Agreement (CAFTA-DR).
2007	The International Court of Justice in the Hague settles a territorial dispute between Honduras and Nicaragua.
2011	Orgeta is re-elected president.
2012	The government evacuates about 3,000 people from the vicinity of the San Cristobal volcano when it begins to erupt.
2014	Nicaragua's constitution is changed, allowing Ortega to run for a third term as president.
2015	Construction of the Grand Nicaraguan Canal begins; the project is expected to take five years to complete.

Booth, John A., et al. *Understanding Central America: Global Forces, Rebellion, and Change,* 5th ed. Boulder, Colo.: Westview Press, 2009.

Egerton, Alex. *Nicaragua.* Oakland, Calif.: Lonely Planet, 2014.

Gritzner, Charles F. *Nicaragua.* New York: Chelsea House, 2010.

Heuman, Gad. *The Caribbean: A Brief History.* New York: Bloomsbury, 2014.

Williamson, Edwin. *The Penguin History of Latin America.* New York: Penguin Group, 2010.

Culture and Festivals

http://www.everyculture.com/Ma-Ni/Nicaragua.html
http://www.lonelyplanet.com/nicaragua

Economic and Political Information

http://www.state.gov/r/pa/ei/bgn/1850.htm
https://www.cia.gov/library/publications/the-world-factbook/geos/nu.html
http://lanic.utexas.edu/

History and Geography

http://www.timeforkids.com/destination/nicaragua/history-timeline
http://web.stanford.edu/group/arts/nicaragua/discovery_eng/history/
http://lcweb2.loc.gov/frd/cs/nitoc.html

Travel information

http://visitnicaragua.us/
http://www.nicaragua.com/

For More Information

American Chamber of Commerce in Nicaragua
Apartado Postal 202
Managua, Nicaragua
Phone: (505) 267-3099

Caribbean/Latin American Action
1625 K Street NW, Suite 200
Washington, DC 20006
Phone: (202) 464-2031
Website: www.c-caa.org

Embassy of Nicaragua
1627 New Hampshire Avenue NW
Washington, D.C. 20009
Phone: (202) 939-6570
Fax: (202) 939-6542

Permanent Representative of Nicaragua to the United Nations
820 Second Avenue, 8th Floor
New York, N.Y. 10017 USA
Phone: (212) 490-7997
Fax: (212) 286-0815
Website: www.un.int/nicaragua
Email: nicaragua@un.int

U.S. Department of Commerce
International Trade Administration
Office of Latin America and the Caribbean
1401 Constitution Ave., NW
Washington, D.C. 20230
Phone: (202) 482-2000
Fax: (202) 482-5168
Website: www.commerce.gov
Email: publicaffairs@doc.gov

U.S. Agency for International Development
Ronald Reagan Building
Washington, D.C. 20523-0001
Phone: (202) 712-0000
Website: www.usaid.gov
Email: pinquiries@usaid.gov

Contributors

Senior Consulting Editor **James D. Henderson** is professor of
international studies at Coastal Carolina University. He is the
author of *Conservative Thought in Twentieth Century Latin America:
The Ideals of Laureano Gómez* (1988; Spanish edition *Las ideas de
Laureano Gómez* published in 1985); *When Colombia Bled: A History
of the Violence in Tolima* (1985; Spanish edition *Cuando Colombia se
desangró, una historia de la Violencia en metrópoli y provincia*, 1984);
and co-author of *A Reference Guide to Latin American History*
(2000) and *Ten Notable Women of Latin America* (1978).

Mr. Henderson earned a bachelors degree in history from Centenary College of
Louisiana, and a masters degree in history from the University of Arizona. He then
spent three years in the Peace Corps, serving in Colombia, before earning his doctorate
in Latin American history in 1972 at Texas Christian University.

Charles J. Shields, the author of all eight books in the
Discovering Central America series, lives in Homewood, a
suburb of Chicago, with his wife Guadalupe, an elementary-
school principal. He has a degree in history from the University
of Illinois in Urbana-Champaign, and was chairman of the
English department and the guidance department at
Homewood-Flossmoor High School in Flossmoor, Illinois.